T0023530

HOW TO THINK ABOUT GOD

ANCIENT WISDOM FOR MODERN READERS

■ ■ ■

HOW TO THINK ABOUT GOD

■ ■ ■ ■ ■

An Ancient Guide for Believers
and Nonbelievers

Marcus Tullius Cicero

*Selected, translated, and introduced
by Philip Freeman*

PRINCETON UNIVERSITY PRESS

PRINCETON AND OXFORD

Published by Princeton University Press
41 William Street, Princeton, New Jersey 08540
6 Oxford Street, Woodstock, Oxfordshire OX20 1TR

press.princeton.edu

ISBN 978-0-691-18365-7

British Library Cataloging-in-Publication Data is available

Editorial: Rob Tempio and Matt Rohal
Production Editorial: Ali Parrington
Text and Jacket Design: Pamela L. Schnitter
Production: Merli Guerra
Publicity: Jodi Price, Amy Stewart, and Alyssa Sanford

Jacket/Cover Credit: Shutterstock

This book has been composed in
Stempel Garamond and Futura

Printed on acid-free paper. ∞

Printed in the United States of America

1 3 5 7 9 10 8 6 4 2

CONTENTS

INTRODUCTION

Ancient Rome was a land full of gods.

Every Roman family honored the ancestral Lares and guardian Penates who watched over their household, as well as Vesta, the goddess who cared for the sacred hearth fire at the center of every home. Beyond the doorway (secured by Janus, who faced both directions) were countless deities of field, stream, and forest. Unlike the Greek gods, these divine spirits rarely had statues or stories connected with them. They were instead forces of nature that animated every corner of the Roman world— and were ignored at one's own peril. Aside from household and nature gods, there were

also state cults devoted to divinities such as Jupiter the lord of the heavens, Mars the god of agriculture (as well as war), and Bona Dea—the good goddess—worshipped only by women.

But as the Romans expanded across the Mediterranean, they met other gods and many new ideas. Foreign divinities were sometimes welcomed into the Roman pantheon, though often with great suspicion, especially those from the exotic East. Cybele, the Great Mother goddess of Asia Minor, came to Rome during the war against Hannibal. The Jews, despite their peculiar notion of a single God, were allowed to worship freely in the city as long as they paid their taxes and caused no trouble.

From the beginning of Roman history there were undoubtedly atheists and skeptics, but it was the encounter with Greek

philosophy that caused many educated Romans to question the religious traditions of their ancestors. Some were intrigued by Pythagoras and his teachings on reincarnation and a mathematical order to the universe. Others were drawn to Plato, a student of Socrates and founder of the Athenian Academy, who taught that there was an invisible world more real than our own and urged a rational quest for the good life. Many, like the Roman poet and philosopher Lucretius, found comfort in the doctrine of Epicurus, who believed the supreme good in life was happiness, with no evidence of divine interest in humanity in a universe made only of atoms. But the most popular brand of Greek philosophy among educated Romans was the Stoicism taught by Zeno and his followers, such as Chrysippus and Posidonius, who believed that

virtue was the supreme good in a materialistic and yet divine universe.

Marcus Tullius Cicero was among those
Romans in the waning years of the Republic who searched for answers beyond the
religion of his forefathers. He loved and
honored the traditions of his homeland, but
they failed to satisfy a deep longing to know
about the role of gods in earthly life, how
the universe was organized, and, perhaps
most of all, whether the human spirit might
survive death.

Cicero had been born in a small Italian
town outside of Rome, but by determina-
tion and an extraordinary mind had risen
in 63 BC to the office of consul, the highest
office in the Roman Republic. His skills
as an orator were unmatched, as were his
talents for compromise and moderation in
an age of political extremes. But in spite of

his best efforts to maintain the role of the Senate in governing the state, the Republic slipped into dictatorship under Julius Caesar, leaving Cicero on the margins if not outright exile more than once during his political career.

It was during these absences from Rome that Cicero devoted himself to study and writing, producing some of the most important political and philosophical writings of the classical age. As he freely admitted, most of his ideas were Greek, but he was no mere copyist. His ability to adapt the teachings of the greatest Greek minds to a broader world influenced not only his own time but readers for centuries to come, from St. Augustine and Dante to Voltaire and Alexander Hamilton.

In 45 BC, the year before Julius Caesar was assassinated, Cicero wrote a number

of important philosophical and rhetorical works including *On the Nature of the Gods* (*De natura deorum*), in which several key figures from Roman history stage an imaginary debate on the proper way to think about the divine. In this long and fascinating book, Velleius the Epicurean argues against the idea of the gods having any interest in human affairs. Balbus the Stoic, in contrast, advocates a view of the universe as a living whole controlled by a divine yet still materialistic God who is the ultimate reality (modern readers may see something similar in the Force of the Star Wars saga). Cotta the Academic, representing the later skeptical teachings developed from Plato, casts both views into doubt. The heart of Balbus's Stoic argument is presented in this volume.

A few years earlier, in 51 BC, Cicero had imitated Plato in writing a book on the

ideals of government. Called *On the Re-public* (*De re publica*), most of the text was lost to modern readers until 1820, when a large part of the book was discovered in the Vatican. Only the conclusion of the book, known as the *Dream of Scipio*, was preserved and studied continuously from antiquity through the Middle Ages and beyond. In this extraordinary dream narrative, given here in its entirety, the Roman hero Scipio is taken on a tour of the heavens by his adoptive grandfather Scipio Africanus. In this nighttime visitation, the younger Scipio discovers the Stoic heavenly design of the universe and the place of a virtuous and eternal soul in it.

Cicero was no religious dogmatist and was indeed a man full of doubts. His own beliefs, reflected in his many treatises and letters, changed repeatedly throughout his

troubled life. At most times he seems to have believed hopefully in the God of the Stoics—though he never identified himself as a Stoic—and the possibility of eternal life for the virtuous. At other periods he appears to have doubted almost everything about religion, including the belief that there was any life beyond the grave. His writings translated in this short volume reflect the more hopeful periods of his life and his preference for the Stoic view of the divine. Unlike his justly celebrated works on friendship and growing older,[1] I present his religious views here for a modern audience not so much for imitation in one's own life as to gain an appreciation for a profound and influential view of the divine just before the dawn of the Christian age.[2]

HOW TO THINK ABOUT GOD

DE NATURA DEORUM
(2.1–44)

1. Quae cum Cotta dixisset, tum Velleius: "Ne ego" inquit "incautus, qui cum Academico et eodem rhetore congredi conatus sim. Nam neque indisertum Academicum pertimuissem nec sine ista philosophia rhetorem quamvis eloquentem; neque enim flumine conturbor inanium verborum nec subtilitate sententiarum si orationis est siccitas. Tu autem, Cotta, utraque re valuisti; corona tibi et iudices defuerunt. Sed ad ista alias, nunc Lucilium, si ipsi commodum est, audiamus."

ON THE NATURE OF THE GODS
(2.1–44)

1. When Cotta had finished speaking, Velleius replied: "I was foolish to try to debate someone who is both an Academic and skilled at rhetoric.[1] I wouldn't have been afraid of an Academic who was a poor speaker nor of an excellent rhetorician who had a poor grasp of philosophy; for I have no fear of a stream of empty, eloquent words nor sharp arguments presented badly. However you, Cotta, are skilled at both! All you lacked was a circle of listeners and a jury. But I'll respond to your criticisms some other time. Let us now hear Lucilius Balbus, if he is willing."

2. Tum Balbus: "Eundem equidem mallem audire Cottam, dum qua eloquentia falsos deos sustulit eadem veros inducat. Est enim et philosophi et pontificis et Cottae de dis inmortalibus habere non errantem et vagam ut Academici sed ut nostri stabilem certamque sententiam. Nam contra Epicurum satis superque dictum est; sed aveo audire tu ipse, Cotta, quid sentias."

"An" inquit "oblitus es quid initio dixerim, facilius me, talibus praesertim de rebus, quid non sentirem, quam quid sentirem posse dicere?

2. Then Balbus spoke: "I would prefer to hear Cotta further, if only he would portray the true gods as eloquently as he has exposed the false. A man like Cotta, who is both a philosopher and a priest, should have a vision of the immortal gods that isn't ambiguous and vague like the Academics but instead sure and certain like what we Stoics hold. We've heard enough and more than enough to disprove the views of the Epicureans. What I'd really like to hear from you now, Cotta, are your own beliefs."

"Surely," Cotta said, "you haven't forgotten what I said at the beginning of our discussion, that it is much easier for me, especially in matters such as these, to talk about what I disbelieve rather than what I believe.

3. "Quod si haberem aliquid quod liqueret, tamen te vicissim audire vellem, cum ipse tam multa dixissem."

Tum Balbus: "Geram tibi morem et agam quam brevissume potero; etenim convictis Epicuri erroribus longa de mea disputatione detracta oratio est. Omnino dividunt nostri totam istam de dis inmortalibus quaestionem in partis quattuor. Primum docent esse deos, deinde quales sint, tum mundum ab his administrari, postremo consulere eos rebus humanis. Nos autem hoc sermone, quae priora duo sunt sumamus; tertium et quartum, quia maiora sunt, puto esse in aliud tempus differenda."

"Minime vero" inquit Cotta "nam et otiosi sumus et his de rebus agimus, quae sunt etiam negotiis anteponenda."

3. "But even if I had something definite to say, I would much rather listen to you in your turn, especially since I've already spoken at length."

Then Balbus replied: "Very well, I will do as you ask as briefly as I can. Since the errors of the Epicureans have already been refuted at length, I can omit much of what I was planning to say.

In general, we Stoics divide the whole question of the immortal gods into four parts: first, we teach that they exist; second, we discuss their nature; third, we show how they govern the universe; and finally, we describe how they care about human affairs. In this present discussion, I think we should focus on the first two points and leave aside the latter two for another time, since they are so vast."

4. Tum Lucilius: "Ne egere quidem videtur" inquit "oratione prima pars. Quid enim potest esse tam apertum tamque perspicuum, cum caelum suspeximus caelestiaque contemplati sumus, quam esse aliquod numen praestantissimae mentis, quo haec regantur? Quod ni ita esset, qui potuisset adsensu omnium dicere Ennius 'aspice hoc sublime candens, quem invocant omnes Iovem'— illum vero et Iovem et dominatorem rerum et omnia motu regentem et, ut idem Ennius, 'patrem divumque hominumque' et praesentem ac praepotentem deum? Quod qui dubitet, haud sane intellego, cur non idem, sol sit an nullus sit, dubitare possit.

"I disagree," said Cotta. "For we have plenty of time and are concerned about questions so important that they should take precedence over any other business."

4. "Very well," said Balbus. "It seems to me that the first point—that the gods exist— scarcely needs discussing. For what could be more clear and obvious when we gaze at the sky and contemplate the heavens, than that there is some divine power of surpassing intelligence which rules over this realm? If this weren't true, how is it that everyone approves of the words of Ennius when he says

> Look up at the shining firmament
> which all call on as Jupiter

and not only as the god Jupiter but as lord of the universe, a present and mighty god,

5. "Qui enim est hoc illo evidentius? Quod nisi cognitum conprehensumque animis haberemus, non tam stabilis opinio permaneret nec confirmaretur diuturnitate temporis nec una cum saeclis aetatibusque hominum inveterare potuisset. Etenim videmus ceteras opiniones fictas atque vanas diuturnitate extabuisse. Quis enim hippocentaurum fuisse aut Chimaeram putat, quaeve anus tam excors inveniri potest quae illa quae quondam credebantur apud inferos portenta

who rules everything by his command? As Ennius calls him:

the father of gods and men.[2]

I can hardly imagine how anyone doubts this. If so, they might as well doubt the existence of the Sun!

5. "For how is the Sun's existence more obvious than that of God? If this idea of the divine was not so clearly known and planted in our minds, would it have endured and become stronger as the centuries passed? How could it have become more steadfast with every succeeding age and generation of humanity? We see that other vain and false beliefs have passed away with time. Who now believes that hippocentaurs or the Chimaera ever existed?[3] Is there any

extimescat? Opinionis enim commenta delet dies, naturae iudicia confirmat.

Itaque et in nostro populo et in ceteris deorum cultus religionumque sanctitates existunt in dies maiores atque meliores.

6. "Idque evenit non temere nec casu, sed quod et praesentes saepe di vim suam declarant, ut et apud Regillum bello Latinorum, cum A. Postumius dictator cum Octavio Mamillio Tusculano proelio dimicaret, in nostra acie Castor et Pollux ex equis pugnare visi sunt, et recentiore memoria idem Tyndaridae Persem victum nuntiaverunt. P. enim Vatinius avus huius adulescentis cum e praefectura Reatina Romam venienti noctu duo iuvenes cum equis albis dixissent regem

ignorant old woman left who still believes in the monsters of the underworld which people once feared? Time erases false beliefs, but confirms the judgments of nature. The result is that among our own people as with others, the worship of the gods and the observance of sacred rites grows stronger and more perfect as time passes.

6. "This doesn't happen randomly nor by chance, but because the gods themselves often make their power known to us. For example, in our war with the Latin League at Lake Regillus, when the dictator Aulus Postumius was battling Octavius Mamilius of Tusculum, Castor and Pollux appeared on horseback on the front lines with our soldiers.[4] More recently these divine sons of Tyndareus appeared to announce the defeat of Perses. Publius Vatinius, the grandfather

Persem illo die captum, <cum> senatui nuntiavisset, primo quasi temere de re publica locutus in carcerem coniectus est, post a Paulo litteris allatis cum idem dies constitisset, et agro a senatu et vacatione donatus est. Atque etiam cum ad fluvium Sagram Crotoniatas Locri maximo proelio devicissent, eo ipso die auditam esse eam pugnam ludis Olympiae memoriae proditum est. Saepe Faunorum voces exauditae, saepe visae formae deorum quemvis aut non hebetem aut impium deos praesentes esse confiteri coegerunt.

of our young contemporary, was traveling to Rome by night from his magistracy at Reate when two young men dressed in white told him that Perses had been captured that very day.[5] When Vatinius announced this to the Senate, he was thrown into jail for making reckless claims about state business. But afterward a letter arrived from Aemilius Paulus confirming victory on that very day, so that the Senate gave Vatinius a grant of public land and special privileges. As another example, when the Locrians soundly defeated the army of the Crotons at the Sagra River, the outcome of the battle, it is said, was heard at the games in Olympia on that same day.[6] Oftentimes voices of fauns have been heard and apparitions of the gods have been seen so that anyone who is not a fool or impious would have to admit that the gods were present.

7. "Praedictiones vero et praesensiones rerum futurarum quid aliud declarant nisi hominibus ea quae sint ostendi, monstrari, portendi, praedici, ex quo illa ostenta, monstra, portenta, prodigia dicuntur. Quod si ea ficta credimus licentia fabularum, Mopsum, Tiresiam, Amphiaraum, Calchantem, Helenum (quos tamen augures ne ipsae quidem fabulae adscivissent, si res omnino repudiarent), ne domesticis quidem exemplis docti numen deorum conprobabimus? Nihil nos P. Clodi bello Punico primo temeritas movebit, qui etiam per iocum deos inridens, cum cavea liberati pulli non pascerentur, mergi eos in aquam iussit, ut biberent, quoniam esse nollent? Qui risus classe devicta multas ipsi lacrimas, magnam populo Romano cladem attulit. Quid collega eius, <L.> Iunius, eodem bello nonne tempestate classem amisit, cum auspiciis non

7. "Then there is the evidence of prophecies and premonitions of things to come. These are proof that the future is being revealed, shown, portended, and foretold to humanity, thus they are called revelations, signs, portents, and predictions. Even if we believe the ancient stories of Mopsus, Teiresias, Amphiaraus, Calchas, and Helenus are mere fictions and fables—although their powers would not have been recognized in fiction unless they had some foundation in fact—will we as learned men dismiss evidence of divine powers if it is from our own recent history?[7] Won't we learn from the outrageous behavior of Publius Claudius in the First Punic War? He mocked the gods as a joke, for when the chickens were released from their cages and refused to eat, he ordered them thrown into the sea, saying they could drink instead. But that jest

paruisset? Itaque Clodius a populo condemnatus est, Iunius necem sibi ipse conscivit.

8. "C. Flaminium Coelius religione neglecta cecidisse apud Transumenum scribit cum magno rei publicae vulnere. Quorum exitio intellegi potest eorum imperiis rem publicam amplificatam, qui religionibus paruissent.

Et si conferre volumus nostra cum externis, ceteris rebus aut pares aut etiam inferiores reperiemur, religione, id est cultu deorum, multo superiores.

led to a great defeat for the fleet of Claudius and a disaster for the Roman people. And didn't his colleague Lucius Junius in the same war lose his ships in a storm because he neglected the auspices?[8] In the end Claudius was condemned by the Roman people and Junius committed suicide.

8. "Coelius records that Gaius Flaminius perished at Trasimene because he neglected religious observances, resulting in grave danger to the Roman Republic.[9] The fate of these men helps us understand that the good of our country was increased when these generals followed religious practices.

Now, if we compare ourselves to other nations, we will find ourselves equal or even inferior in some respects—but not in religion, that is, the worship of the gods, in which we are far superior.

9. "An Atti Navi lituus ille, quo ad investigandum suem regiones vineae terminavit, contemnendus est? Crederem, nisi eius augurio rex Hostilius maxima bella gessisset. Sed neglegentia nobilitatis augurii disciplina omissa veritas auspiciorum spreta est, species tantum retenta; itaque maximae rei publicae partes, in is bella quibus rei publicae salus continetur, nullis auspiciis administrantur, nulla peremnia servantur, nulla ex acuminibus, nulli viri vocantur, ex quo in procinctu testamenta perierunt; tum enim bella gerere nostri duces incipiunt, cum auspicia posuerunt.

9. "Or should we laugh at the augural staff of Attus Navius, who used it to trace out the sections of his vineyard to find his lost pig?[10] I would believe laughter justified except that King Tullus Hostilius called on his services as an augur before he waged great wars. But nowadays our leaders have abandoned the art of augury and no longer believe in the truth auspices teach, continuing only the empty forms. And so the greatest affairs of state, including the wars that ensure our safety, are conducted without taking the auspices. We no longer call on the gods when crossing rivers nor when our spears flash nor when men are called up for service. Soldiers no longer write their wills before going into battle and generals wage war without first conducting the auspices.

10. "At vero apud maiores tanta religionis vis fuit, ut quidam imperatores etiam se ipsos dis inmortalibus capite velato verbis certis pro re publica devoverent. Multa ex Sibyllinis vaticinationibus, multa ex haruspicum responsis commemorare possum quibus ea confirmentur, quae dubia nemini debent esse. Atqui et nostrorum augurum et Etruscorum haruspicum disciplinam P. Scipione C. Figulo consulibus res ipsa probavit. quos cum Ti. Gracchus consul iterum crearet, primus rogator, ut eos rettulit, ibidem est repente mortuus. Gracchus cum comitia nihilo minus peregisset remque illam in religionem populo venisse sentiret, ad senatum rettulit. Senatus quos ad soleret, referendum censuit. Haruspices introducti responderunt non fuisse iustum comitiorum rogatorem.

10. "Truly the power of religious feelings was so strong in the past that some of our generals even devoted themselves to the immortal gods, with heads veiled and formal prayers recited, for the good of our country.[11] I could recount many examples of Sibylline prophecies or words from soothsayers, the fulfillment of which no one ought to doubt. But instead let me remind you of the truth of augury and the divine power of Etruscan soothsayers by recalling the events that occurred in the consulship of Publius Scipio and Gaius Figulus.[12]

Tiberius Gracchus was presiding over their election during his second consulship when suddenly the senior voting official dropped dead just as he was announcing their names. Gracchus nonetheless went through with the election. Later he realized

11. "Tum Gracchus, ut e patre audiebam, incensus ira: 'Itane vero, ego non iustus, qui et consul rogavi et augur et auspicato? an vos Tusci ac barbari auspiciorum populi Romani ius tenetis et interpretes esse comitiorum potestis?' Itaque tum illos exire iussit. Post autem e provincia litteras ad collegium misit, se cum legeret libros recordatum esse vitio sibi tabernaculum captum fuisse hortos Scipionis, quod, cum pomerium postea intrasset habendi senatus causa,

that the unusual proceedings had troubled the religious sensibilities of the common people, so he referred the matter to the Senate. The Senate then referred it to the usual religious officers for consideration. These Etruscan soothsayers responded that the incorrect appointment of the official who had died made the elections invalid.

11. "My own father told me that Gracchus was furious at this ruling and shouted: 'What? How could I have been out of order when I myself, being both consul and augur, had taken the proper auspices? Are you barbaric Etruscans really going to be the arbiters of what is right concerning the auspices of the Roman people and what is valid in how we conduct our elections?' Then he threw them out of the Senate chambers. But afterward he sent a letter to

in redeundo cum idem pomerium transiret auspicari esset oblitus; itaque vitio creatos consules esse. Augures rem ad senatum; senatus ut abdicarent consules; abdicaverunt.

Quae quaerimus exempla maiora: vir sapientissimus atque haud sciam an omnium praestantissimus peccatum suum, quod celari posset, confiteri maluit quam haerere in re publica religionem, consules summum imperium statim deponere quam id tenere punctum temporis contra religionem.

the College of Augurs from his province stating that, after consulting the augural books, he realized he had been mistaken in choosing the Gardens of Scipio as the site of his tent for taking the auspices before the election. For he had subsequently crossed the boundary of Rome to hold a meeting of the Senate, then had omitted taking the auspices at the city limit on his return journey. Thus, he said, the election of the consuls had been invalid. The augurs then sent word to the Senate, which informed the elected consuls, who immediately resigned.

Do we need a better example than this? Here we have one of our wisest leaders, perhaps the most eminent man of all, confessing he had made a mistake—which, by the way, he could have easily concealed. But he preferred to admit his behavior was

12. "Magna augurum auctoritas; quid haruspicum ars nonne divina? Haec <et> in-
numerabilia ex eodem genere qui videat
nonne cogatur confiteri deos esse? Quorum
enim interpretes sunt, eos ipsos esse certe
necesse est; deorum autem interpretes sunt;
deos igitur esse fateamur. At fortasse non
omnia eveniunt, quae praedicta sunt. Ne
aegri quidem quia non omnes convalescunt,
idcirco ars nulla medicina est. Signa ostend-
untur a dis rerum futurarum; in his si qui
erraverunt, non deorum natura, sed hominum coniectura peccavit.

wrong rather than allow a religious error to harm the Republic. And the elected consuls preferred to lay down the highest power granted by the state rather than risk offending the gods.

12. "The authority of augurs is great; and surely shouldn't we grant that the art of soothsayers is divine? Wouldn't anyone who acknowledges my previous examples and countless others of the same sort have to confess that the gods exist? Whenever people employ spokesmen, those people by necessity exist. The gods have spokesmen, therefore we must agree that the gods exist. Perhaps someone might say that not all predictions turn out to be true. But we wouldn't say that because not all sick people get better there is no art of medicine.

Itaque inter omnis omnium gentium summa constat; omnibus enim innatum est et in animo quasi inscriptum esse deos.

13. "Quales sint, varium est, esse nemo negat. Cleanthes quidem noster quattuor de causis dixit in animis hominum informatas deorum esse notiones, primam posuit eam, de qua modo dixi, quae orta esset ex praesensione rerum futurarum; alteram, quam ceperimus ex magnitudine commodorum, quae percipiuntur caeli temperatione, fecunditate terrarum aliarumque commoditatum complurium copia.

The gods give us signs of things yet to come; if some spokesman errs in interpreting these, the fault lies not with the nature of the gods but with human interpretation.

And so concerning this there is agreement among all people of every nation. It is, so to speak, engraved from birth in the hearts of us all that the gods exist.

13. "Concerning what the gods are like, there are many opinions—but no one denies that they exist. Cleanthes of our Stoic tradition said there are four ways in which the nature of the gods is made known to our souls.[13] The first, which I just now discussed, arises from the foreknowledge of future events. The second, we perceive from the abundant benefits that come to us from our temperate climate, the fertility of the Earth, and many other blessings.

14. "Tertiam quae terreret animos fulminibus, tempestatibusn, nimbis, nivibus, grandinibus, vastitate, pestilentia, terrae motibus et saepe fremitibus lapideisque imbribus et guttis imbrium quasi cruentis, tum labibus aut repentinis terrarum hiatibus, tum praeter naturam hominum pecudumque portentis, tum facibus visis caelestibus, tum stellis—is quas Graeci *kometas*, nostri cincinnatas vocant, quae nuper bello Octaviano magnarum fuerunt calamitatum praenuntiae—tum sole geminato, quod, ut e patre audivi, Tuditano et Aquilio consulibus evenerat, quo quidem anno P. Africanus, sol alter, extinctus est, quibus exterriti homines vim quandam esse caelestem et diviam suspicati sunt.

14. "The third method of divine revelation is from the terror we feel in our souls from lightning, storms, downpours of rain, snow, hail, devastation, plague, and earthquakes, as well as from rumblings of the ground, showers of stones, and raindrops as red as blood. Then there are the sudden openings and fissures in the earth, along with unnatural prodigies both human and animal, fires in the heavens, and what the Greeks call *comets* but we refer to as long-tailed stars. These appeared foretelling great calamity in the recent war conducted by Octavius.[14] There was also the appearance of twin suns, as my father told me, during the consulship of Tuditanus and Aquilius, in the year Publius Africanus died, himself another sun.[15] These events terrified people and made them believe some divine and heavenly power was at work.

15. "Quartam causam esse eamque vel max-
imam aequabilitatem motus <constantissi-
mamque> conversionem caeli, solis lunae
siderumque omnium distinctionem, utili-
tatem, pulchritudinem, ordinem, quarum
rerum aspectus ipse satis indicaret non esse
ea fortuita: ut, si quis in domum aliquam aut
in gymnasium aut in forum venerit, cum
videat omnium rerum rationem, modum,
disciplinam, non possit ea sine causa fieri
iudicare, sed esse aliquem intellegat, qui
praesit et cui pareatur, multo magis in tantis motionibus tantisque vicissitudinibus,
tam multarum rerum atque tantarum or-
dinibus, in quibus nihil umquam inmensa et
infinita vetustas mentita sit, statuat necesse
est ab aliqua mente tantos naturae motus
gubernari.

15. "The fourth and best reason Cleanthes puts forward for knowledge of the gods is the uniform and constant movement of the heavens, that is, the variety, usefulness, beauty, and order of the Sun, Moon, and all the stars. The evidence of these celestial bodies should be enough to prove they are not the result of chance. Suppose that someone enters a home or gymnasium or public square and sees that everything there is well-ordered, systematic, and organized. Wouldn't he be able to rightly judge that this was not an accident but the result of an intelligent mind at work whose orders are obeyed? Shouldn't we assume an even greater mind at work when we turn our eyes to the heavens and see such vast and profound movements, such an immense and innumerable order, which never in the long and countless ages past has deviated?

16. "Chrysippus quidem, quamquam est acerrimo ingenio, tamen ea dicit, ut ab ipsa natura didicisse, non ut ipse repperisse videatur. 'Si enim' inquit 'est aliquid in rerum natura quod hominis mens, quod ratio, quod vis, quod potestas humana efficere non possit, est certe id, quod illud efficit, homine melius; atqui res caelestes omnesque eae, quarum est ordo sempiternus, ab homine confici non possunt; est igitur id, quo illa conficiuntur, homine melius. Id autem quid potius dixeris quam deum? Etenim si di non sunt, quid esse potest in rerum natura homine melius; in eo enim solo est ratio, qua nihil potest esse praestantius; esse autem hominem, qui nihil in omni mundo melius esse quam se putet,

Shouldn't we confess that some mind controls these movements of nature?

16. "Chrysippus had a formidable intelligence, but what he says about these things seems not to have come from himself but learned from nature herself:[16] 'If there is anything in nature that the human mind and reason or human strength and power cannot achieve, it is certain that such a thing must have been created by something superior to man. Now, the heavenly bodies in their eternal order cannot have been created by man. Therefore, that which created them is superior to man. What would we call this creator other than God? Indeed, if gods do not exist, then there is nothing in nature greater than humans, for we alone possess reason, which is greater than any other ability. For humans to exist in this universe

desipientis adrogantiae est; ergo est aliquid melius. Est igitur profecto deus.

17. "'An vero, si domum magnam pulchramque videris, non possis adduci ut, etiam si dominum non videas, muribus illam et mustelis aedificatam putes: tantum ergo ornatum mundi, tantam varietatem pulchritudinemque rerum caelestium, tantam vim et magnitudinem maris atque terrarum si tuum ac non deorum inmortalium domicilium putes, nonne plane desipere videare?

An ne hoc quidem intellegimus omnia supera esse meliora, terram autem esse infimam, quam crassissimus circumfundat aer: ut ob eam ipsam causam, quod etiam quibusdam regionibus atque urbibus contingere videmus, hebetiora ut sint hominum

thinking nothing is greater than themselves is foolishly arrogant. Therefore, there is something superior. And thus God certainly exists.

17. " 'Suppose,' continues Chrysippus, 'that you see a large and beautiful house. Even if the architect wasn't immediately visible, no one could convince you that it was built by mice and weasels. So then if you examined the order of the universe with its great celestial variety and beauty, along with all the power and majesty of the sea and lands, and then assumed that this was your house rather than that of the immortal gods, wouldn't you be out of your mind?

And don't we understand that all things that are higher are better? But the Earth is lowest of all, surrounded by a thick layer of air. Because of this, what we see in some

ingenia propter caeli pleniorem naturam, hoc idem generi humano evenerit, quod in terra hoc est in crassissima regione mundi conlocati sint.

18. " 'Et tamen ex ipsa hominum sollertia esse aliquam mentem et eam quidem acriorem et divinam existimare debemus. Unde enim hanc homo arripuit ut ait apud Xenophontem Socrates. Quin et umorem et calorem, qui est fusus in corpore, et terrenam ipsam viscerum soliditatem, animum denique illum spirabilem si quis quaerat unde habeamus apparet; quorum aliud a terra sumpsimus aliud ab umore aliud ab igni aliud ab aere eo quem spiritum dicimus. Illud autem quod vincit haec omnia,

particular lands and cities with dense atmospheres in regard to the slow-witted nature of their citizens is true on a broader scale for the whole human race, because we all live on the Earth, in the densest region of the universe.[17]

18. " 'In spite of our limitations, the human intelligence we possess ought to lead us to reason that there exists another mind greater than our own—one that is in fact divine. Otherwise, as Socrates asks in the pages of Xenophon,[18] where did we acquire the minds we have? If someone asks where we get the moisture and heat defused throughout our bodies or the earthly substance of our own flesh or finally the breath of life within us, the answer is clear: one comes from the earth, another from water,

rationem dico et, si placet pluribus verbis, mentem, consilium, cogitationem, pruden- tiam, ubi invenimus unde sustulimus? An cetera mundus habebit omnia, hoc unum, quod plurimi est, non habebit? Atqui certe nihil omnium rerum melius est mundo nihil praestantius nihil pulchrius, nec solum nihil est, sed ne cogitari quidem quicquam me- lius potest. Et si ratione et sapientia nihil est melius, necesse est haec inesse in eo quod optimum esse concedimus.

19. "'Quid vero tanta rerum consentiens, conspirans, continuata cognatio quem non

still another from fire, and the last, which we call breath, from the air.[19] But that quality we have that surpasses all of these, which I call reason—though you may also call it intelligence, deliberation, thought, or wisdom—where did we discover or obtain that? Is it possible that the universe contains these other qualities but not that one thing which is greater than all the rest? Now, it is certain that there is nothing greater than the universe. Not only is there nothing superior and more beautiful, but we can't even conceive of anything beyond it. Therefore, if there is no human quality better than reason or wisdom, it must also exist in that which we have agreed is the grandest thing of all.

19. " 'Consider also the harmony, connection, and continuity of all things. Won't this

coget ea quae dicuntur a me conprobare? Possetne uno tempore florere, dein vicissim horrere terra, aut tot rebus ipsis se inmutantibus solis accessus discessusque solstitiis brumisque cognosci, aut aestus maritimi fretorumque angustiae ortu aut obitu lunae commoveri, aut una totius caeli conversione cursus astrorum dispares conservari? Haec ita fieri omnibus inter se concinentibus mundi partibus profecto non possent, nisi ea uno divino et continuato spiritu continerentur.'

20. "Atque haec cum uberius disputantur et fusius, ut mihi est in animo facere, facilius effugiunt Academicorum calumniam; cum autem, ut Zeno solebat, brevius angustiusque

compel everyone to agree with what I say? How can the earth in one season blossom with flowers and then become barren? How can the coming and going of the Sun at the summer and winter solstices signal the changes that take place in so many things around us? How can the tides of the sea and the waters in narrow straits be moved by the rising and setting of the Moon? How can the various courses of the stars be maintained in a single revolution of the heavens? These processes and all the harmonious works of the universe could not take place unless they were held together by one divine and all-pervading spirit.'

20. "When these arguments are presented in a more full and flowing and style, as I intend to do, it's easier to avoid the baseless criticisms of the Academic philosophers. But

concluduntur, tum apertiora sunt ad repren-
dendum, nam ut profluens amnis aut vix
aut nullo modo, conclusa autem aqua facile
conrumpitur, sic orationis flumine repren-
soris convicia diluuntur, angustia autem
conclusae rationis non facile se ipsa tutatur.
Haec enim quae dilatantur a nobis Zeno sic
premebat:

21. "'Quod ratione utitur id melius est
quam id quod ratione non utitur; nihil
autem mundo melius; ratione igitur mundus utitur.' Similiter effici potest sapientem
esse mundum, similiter beatum, similiter
aeternum; omnia enim haec meliora sunt
quam ea quae sunt his carentia, nec mundo
quicquam melius. Ex quo efficietur esse
mundum deum.

when these ideas are put forward quite briefly and tersely as Zeno used to do, then they are more open to criticism.[20] A running river suffers little or no pollution, but an enclosed pool is easily sullied. Likewise critics are easily diluted by a stream of eloquence, whereas the narrow confines of a closely reasoned argument leave little room for defense. My rather expansive arguments were compressed by Zeno into the following form:

21. " 'That which uses reason is superior to that which does not. Nothing is superior to the universe. Therefore the universe uses reason.'

Using a similar argument we could also argue that the universe is wise and blessed and eternal. For all things that have these qualities are superior to those things that lack them—and nothing is superior to the

22. "Idemque hoc modo: 'Nullius sensu carentis pars aliqua potest esse sentiens; mundi autem partes sentientes sunt; non igitur caret sensu mundus.' Pergit idem et urguet angustius: 'Nihil' inquit 'quod animi quodque rationis est expers, id generare ex se potest animantem compotemque rationis; mundus autem generat animantis compotesque rationis; animans est igitur mundus composque rationis.' Idemque similitudine, ut saepe solet, rationem conclusit hoc modo: 'Si ex oliva modulate canentes tibiae nascerentur, num dubitares quin inesset in oliva tibicini quaedam scientia? Quid si platani fidiculas ferrent numerose sonantes: idem scilicet censeres in platanis inesse musicam, cur igitur mundus non animans

universe. Thus it follows that the universe is God.

22. "Zeno continues like this: 'Nothing lacking in sensation can have a part of itself with sensation. Parts of the universe, however, do have sensation; therefore the universe cannot be lacking in sensation.' He goes on to argue in a more narrow way: 'Nothing without spirit and reason can give birth to an animate and reasoning being. The universe, however, generates animate and rational beings; therefore the universe itself must be animate and rational.' Zeno concludes his argument by using similes, one of his favorite techniques: 'If you saw sprouting from an olive tree flutes that were playing beautifully, would you doubt that contained inside that olive tree was a knowledge of flute-playing? If you saw a plane

sapiensque iudicetur, cum ex se procreet animantis atque sapientis?'

23. "Sed quoniam coepi secus agere atque initio dixeram—negaram enim hanc primam partem egere oratione, quod esset omnibus perspicuum deos esse—tamen id ipsum rationibus physicis, id est naturalibus, confirmari volo. Sic enim res se habet, ut omnia, quae alantur et quae crescant, contineant in se vim caloris, sine qua neque ali possent nec crescere. Nam omne quod est calidum et igneum cietur et agitur motu suo; quod autem alitur et crescit motu quodam utitur certo et aequabili; qui quam diu remanet in nobis, tam diu sensus et vita remanet,

tree bearing lutes playing beautiful tunes, wouldn't you believe likewise that plane trees possessed the art of music? Why then is the universe not judged to be animate and wise when it produces creatures that are animate and wise?'

23. "But even though I have begun to wander from the way I dealt with this question at the beginning of my discussion—for I said then that this first part required no proof since the existence of God should be clear to everyone—nonetheless I would like to press home my point with arguments drawn from physics, that is, from the natural world. It is clear that everything which is nourished and grows contains within itself the power of heat, for without heat nothing could live or grow. For everything that is hot and fiery by nature is driven and

refrigerato autem et extincto calore occidimus ipsi et extinguimur.

24. "Quod quidem Cleanthes his etiam argumentis docet, quanta vis insit caloris in omni corpore: negat enim esse ullum cibum tam gravem, quin is nocte et die concoquatur; cuius etiam in reliquiis inest calor iis, quas natura respuerit. Iam vero venae et arteriae micare non desinunt quasi quodam igneo motu, animadversumque saepe est, cum cor animantis alicuius evolsum ita mobiliter palpitaret, ut imitaretur igneam celeritatem. Omne igitur, quod vivit, sive

sustained by its own movement. Indeed, everything that is nourished and grows possesses a steady and uniform motion. As long as this motion remains within us, sensation and life remain. But when this heat grows cold and fades away, we ourselves die and are extinguished.

24. "Cleanthes also teaches this same doctrine with further arguments to demonstrate how great is the power of heat in every living body. He says that no food is so solid that it can't be digested in a night and a day; and that even the residue nature rejects which passes from our bodies contains heat. He also states that the veins and arteries of living creatures never cease throbbing with a fiery motion. Indeed, it often happens that when the heart is ripped from

animal, sive terra editum, id vivit propter
inclusum in eo calorem, ex quo intellegi
debet eam caloris naturam vim habere in se
vitalem per omnem mundum pertinentem.

25. "Atque id facilius cernemus toto genere hoc igneo, quod tranat omnia subtilius
explicato. Omnes igitur partes mundi (tan-
gam autem maximas) calore fultae susti-
nentur. Quod primum in terrena natura
perspici potest. Nam et lapidum conflictu
atque tritu elici ignem videmus et recenti
fossione terram fumare calentem, atque
etiam ex puteis iugibus aquam calidam trahi,
et id maxime fieri temporibus hibernis,
quod magna vis terrae cavernis contineatur
caloris eaque hieme sit densior ob eamque

some animal, it continues to beat so quickly that it resembles a flickering fire. Therefore, every living thing, whether animal or plant, lives because of the heat contained within it. From this we should conclude that elemental heat possesses a vital force within it that extends throughout the whole universe.

25. "We can understand this more easily if we explain in greater detail the whole element of fire which pervades everything. All parts of the universe—though I will mention only the most important—are sustained and supported by heat. This can be seen first of all in the element of earth. We observe fire produced when rocks are struck or rubbed together, and when earth freshly dug steams with warmth. Note also that water drawn from springs is warm, especially in winter, because there is a

causam calorem insitum in terris contineat
artius.

26. "Longa est oratio multaeque rationes,
quibus doceri possit omnia, quae terra con-
cipiat, semina quaeque ipsa ex se generata
stirpibus infixa contineat ea temperatione
caloris et oriri et augescere. Atque aquae
etiam admixtum esse calorem primum ipse
liquor aquae declarat et fusio, quae neque
conglaciaret frigoribus neque nive pruin-
aque concresceret, nisi eadem se admixto
calore liquefacta et dilapsa diffunderet;
itaque et aquilonibus reliquisque frigoribus adiectis durescit umor, et idem vicissim
mollitur tepefactus et tabescit calore. Atque
etiam maria agitata ventis ita tepescunt, ut
intellegi facile possit in tantis illis umoribus

great concentration of heat in underground caverns—for in winter the earth grows more dense and compresses even more the heat stored within it.

26. "It would require a lengthy discussion and a great host of arguments to show that the seeds the earth holds within her womb and the plants she spontaneously generates that fix their roots in her all owe their origin and growth to the warmth she contains.

As for water, it's easy to see that its changeable nature demonstrates first of all that heat is mixed within it. It would not freeze into ice in winter nor congeal into snow or frost unless it could also become thawed and liquefied by the mixing in of heat. This is why water solidifies when cold winds from the north or some other quarter blow, and why it softens when warmed

esse inclusum calorem; nec enim ille externus et adventicius habendus est tepor, sed ex intumis maris partibus agitatione excitatus, quod nostris quoque corporibus contingit, cum motu atque exercitatione recalescunt. Ipse vero aer, qui natura est maxime frigidus, minime est expers caloris.

27. "Ille vero et multo quidem calore admixtus est: ipse enim oritur ex respiratione aquarum; earum enim quasi vapor quidam aer habendus est, is autem existit motu eius caloris, qui aquis continetur, quam similitudinem cernere possumus in his aquis, quae effervescunt subiectis ignibus. Iam vero

and evaporates with heat. The seas also become warm when stirred by winds, so that we can conclude these massive waters contain heat. We should not think that warmth enters the waters from the outside but that heat is stirred up from the depths of the sea by violent motion, just as our bodies become warm through movement and exercise.

Air likewise, though by nature the coldest of the elements, is not devoid of heat.

27. "Indeed there is much heat mixed with air, for air itself is generated by an exhalation from the waters. Air is actually a kind of vaporized water caused by the motion of heat contained within the waters. We can see something similar happening when water is placed on a fire and begins to boil.

reliqua quarta pars mundi: ea et ipsa tota natura fervida est et ceteris naturis omnibus salutarem inpertit et vitalem calorem.

28. "Ex quo concluditur, cum omnes mundi partes sustineantur calore, mundum etiam ipsum simili parique natura in tanta diuturnitate servari, eoque magis, quod intellegi debet calidum illud atque igneum ita in omni fusum esse natura, ut in eo insit procreandi vis et causa gignendi, a quo et animantia omnia et ea, quorum stirpes terra continentur, et nasci sit necesse et augescere.

29. "Natura est igitur, quae contineat mundum omnem eumque tueatur, et ea quidem

There remains a fourth part of the universe which by its nature is wholly composed of fire, bestowing health and life-giving heat on all the other elements in nature.

28. "From this we should conclude that since all parts of the universe are sustained by heat, this heat—or something similar to it—has preserved the universe through all the ages. Even more, we should see that this hot and fiery substance is infused with all of nature, so that in it is the force of procreation and the very cause of bringing into existence. It is indeed the source of birth and growth for all living things, whether animals or plants rooted in the earth.

29. "There is therefore an element that holds the whole universe together and protects

non sine sensu atque ratione. Omnem enim naturam necesse est, quae non solitaria sit neque simplex sed cum alio iuncta atque conexa, habere aliquem in se principatum, ut in homine mentem, in belua quiddam simile mentis, unde oriantur rerum adpetitus; in arborum autem et earum rerum, quae gignuntur e terra, radicibus inesse principatus putatur, principatum autem id dico, quod Graeci *hegemonikon* vocant, quo nihil in quoque genere nec potest nec debet esse praestantius, ita necesse est illud etiam, in quo sit totius naturae principatus, esse omnium optumum omniumque rerum potestate dominatuque dignissimum.

it—an element not without sensation and reason. For every element in nature—provided it is not solitary and simple but instead complex and joined with other parts—must have within it some ruling principle. In human beings this principle is the mind, while in animals it is something similar to the mind which awakens their desire for things. In trees and plants which grow from the earth, this ruling principle is thought to reside in their roots.[21]

In Latin I use the term *principatus* for this, whereas in Greek it is *hegemonikon*, meaning that force in each kind of thing over which nothing can have more power. From this it must follow that the element containing the ruling principle of the whole of nature is the best of all things and is worthy of power and dominion over all things.

30. "Videmus autem in partibus mundi (nihil est enim in omni mundo, quod non pars universi sit) inesse sensum atque rationem. In ea parte igitur, in qua mundi inest principatus, haec inesse necessest, et acriora quidem atque maiora. Quocirca sapientem esse mundum necesse est, naturamque eam, quae res omnes conplexa teneat, perfectione rationis excellere, eoque deum esse mundum omnemque vim mundi natura divina contineri.

31. "Atque etiam mundi ille fervor purior perlucidior mobiliorque multo ob easque causas aptior ad sensus commovendos quam hic noster calor, quo haec, quae nota nobis sunt, retinentur et vigent. Absurdum igitur est dicere, cum homines bestiaeque hoc

30. "So we see how parts of the universe—and there is nothing in the universe that is not a part of it—possess sensation and reason. It follows therefore that the part of the universe which possesses the ruling principle must also have these qualities, but in a keener and greater form. Thus we can assume that the universe must possess wisdom and that the element which holds together all that exists excels in perfect reason. From this we see that the universe is in fact God and that the vital force of the universe is held together by this divine nature.

31. "Moreover, the fiery heat of the universe is more pure, more radiant, and by far more mobile and thus more stimulating to our senses than the heat by which we experience all things we know that are preserved and brought to life. Therefore it is absurd

calore teneantur et propterea moveantur ac
sentiant, mundum esse sine sensu, qui in-
tegro et libero et puro eodemque acerrimo
et mobilissimo ardore teneatur, praesertim
cum is ardor qui est mundi non agitatus ab
alio neque externo pulsu sed per se ipse ac
sua sponte moveatur; nam quid potest esse
mundo valentius, quod pellat atque moveat
calorem eum, quo ille teneatur.

32. "Audiamus enim Platonem quasi quendam deum philosophorum; cui duo placet
esse motus, unum suum, alterum externum,
esse autem divinius, quod ipsum ex se sua
sponte moveatur quam, quod pulsu agitetur

to say—since both humans and beasts are maintained by this heat and thereby move and have feelings—that the universe is without sensation, possessed as it is by a heat that is vigorous, free, and pure, as well as supremely keen and mobile. This argument is made stronger by fact that the primal heat of the universe does not derive its motion from some force outside itself, but is spontaneously moved by itself. For how can there be anything more powerful than the universe? What else could provide impetus and movement to the heat by which the universe is held together?

32. "We should listen to Plato, who is almost a god among philosophers. He says that there are two kinds of motion, one self-originating, the other derived from something external.[22] That motion which is self-

alieno. Hunc autem motum in solis animis esse ponit, ab isque principium motus esse ductum putat. Quapropter, quoniam ex mundi ardore motus omnis oritur, is autem ardor non alieno inpulsu, sed sua sponte movetur, animus sit necesse est; ex quo efficitur animantem esse mundum.

Atque ex hoc quoque intellegi poterit in eo inesse intellegentiam, quod certe est mundus melior quam ulla natura. Ut enim nulla pars est corporis nostri, quae non minoris sit quam nosmet ipsi sumus, sic mundum universum pluris esse necesse est quam partem aliquam universi. Quod si ita est, sapiens sit mundus necesse est, nam ni ita esset, hominem, qui esset mundi pars, quoniam rationis esset particeps, pluris esse quam mundum omnem oporteret.

originating is more divine than that which has its motion imposed on it from outside itself. The former motion he attributes only to souls, from which he believes all motion arises. Since all motion originates in the primal heat of the universe and since that heat is self-originating and not moved by something external, it follows that the universal heat is a living soul. In other words, the universe itself is alive.

Another argument that the universe possesses intelligence is that it is without a doubt better than any of its parts. Just as there is no part of our body that is not less than our whole self, so too the universe must be greater than any portion of itself. It follows then that the universe must be wise, for if it weren't, then rational human beings—who are a part of it—would be greater than the entire universe.

33. "Atque etiam si a primis incohatisque naturis ad ultimas perfectasque volumus procedere, ad deorum naturam perveniamus necesse est. Prima enim animadvertimus a natura sustineri ea, quae gignantur e terra, quibus natura nihil tribuit amplius quam, ut ea alendo atque augendo tueretur.

34. "Bestiis autem sensum et motum dedit et cum quodam adpetitu accessum ad res salutares a pestiferis recessum, hoc homini amplius, quod addidit rationem, qua regerentur animi adpetitus, qui tum remitterentur, tum continerentur. Quartus autem est gradus et altissimus eorum, qui natura boni sapientesque gignuntur, quibus a principio innascitur ratio recta constansque,

33. "Another proof is this: If we wish to proceed from the primal and most undeveloped levels of being to the highest and most perfect, we will by necessity arrive at the nature of the gods. First we see at the lowest levels that nature sustains those plants which spring from the earth. To them, she gives nothing more than her care in nurturing and growth.

34. "To animals, however, nature has given feeling and movement, along with a certain desire to seek that which is good for them and to avoid that which is harmful. To humans, she has given something more with the addition of reason, so that we might rule over the appetites of our nature, sometimes indulging them and at other times holding back. But there is a fourth and highest kind

quae supra hominem putanda est deoque tribuenda, id est mundo, in quo necesse est perfectam illam atque absolutam inesse rationem.

35. "Neque enim dici potest in ulla rerum institutione non esse aliquid extremum atque perfectum, ut enim in vite, ut in pecude, nisi, quae vis obstitit, videmus natu-ram suo quodam itinere ad ultimum perve-nire, atque ut pictura et fabrica ceteraeque artes habent quendam absoluti operis ef-fectum, sic in omni natura ac multo etiam magis necesse est absolvi aliquid ac perfici. Etenim ceteris naturis multa externa, quo minus perficiantur, possunt obsistere, uni-versam autem naturam nulla res potest im-pedire propterea, quod omnis naturas ipsa

of being born by nature good and wise, endowed from the beginning with right and constant reasoning. This level is higher than humanity and must be assigned to God — that is, to the universe — which by necessity possesses perfect and absolute reason.

35. "Indeed it cannot be denied that in every component of the universe there is a striving for ultimate perfection. For example, in vines or cattle we see that nature will proceed along her own path to the goal of completeness unless some outside force intervenes. We know that with painting or architecture or other arts, there is an idea of perfect workmanship. Even more so with nature as a whole it is necessary that there must be some process of moving toward completion and perfection. Of course, the many individual parts of nature at times

cohibet et continet. Quocirca necesse est esse quartum illum et altissimum gradum, quo nulla vis possit accedere.

36. "Is autem est gradus, in quo rerum omnium natura ponitur; quae quoniam talis est, ut et praesit omnibus et eam nulla res possit inpedire, necesse est intellegentem esse mundum et quidem etiam sapientem.

Quid autem est inscitius quam eam naturam, quae omnis res sit conplexa, non optumam dici, aut, cum sit optuma, non primum animantem esse, deinde rationis et consilii compotem, postremo sapientem. qui enim potest aliter esse optima? Neque enim, si stirpium similis sit aut etiam bestiarum,

encounter obstacles which block their path to perfect realization of their potential, but it cannot be that nature as a whole can be frustrated, since she embodies and contains all things. This is why the fourth and highest level must exist, so that no external force can approach it.

36. "It is on this fourth level that the nature of all things rests. Since this level is such that it presides over everything and nothing is able to impede it, it necessarily follows that the universe is intelligent and indeed wise.

What could be more ignorant than to say that nature—which embraces all things—is not the best of all things? Or, if someone concedes it is in fact best, to say that it is not, first of all, alive? Or perhaps someone will go on to deny that it has reason and

optuma putanda sit potius quam deter-
ruma. Nec vero, si rationis particeps sit nec
sit tamen a principio sapiens, non sit deterior mundi potius quam humana condicio.
Homo enim sapiens fieri potest, mundus
autem, si in aeterno praeteriti temporis
spatio fuit insipiens, numquam profecto
sapientiam consequetur; ita erit homine
deterior. Quod quoniam absurdum est, et
sapiens a principio mundus et deus habendus est.

37. "Neque enim est quicquam aliud praeter
mundum quoi nihil absit quodque undique

purpose? Or finally, will someone say that nature isn't in fact wise at all? How else can it possibly be best? For if nature simply resembles plants or even animals, it can't be thought of as highest on the scale of beings but instead lowest. Even if someone were to grant that the universe had some share of reason but had not been wise from the beginning, it would still clearly be inferior to human beings, for a human is able to become wise. But the universe, if it lacked wisdom at some point of time in the past, will never become wise. That would make it inferior to human beings, which is clearly absurd. We must therefore agree that the universe was wise and divine from the beginning.

37. "Indeed there is nothing aside from the universe that lacks nothing. It is fully

aptum atque perfectum expletumque sit omnibus suis numeris et partibus. Scite enim Chrysippus, ut clipei causa involucrum vaginam autem gladii, sic praeter mundum cetera omnia aliorum causa esse generata, ut eas fruges atque fructus, quos terra gignit, animantium causa, animantes autem hominum, ut ecum vehendi causa, arandi bovem, venandi et custodiendi canem; ipse autem homo ortus est ad mundum contemplandum et imitandum—nullo modo perfectus, sed est quaedam particula perfecti.

38. "Sed mundus quoniam omnia conplexus est neque est quicquam, quod non insit in eo, perfectus undique est; qui igitur potest ei desse id, quod est optimum? Nihil autem est mente et ratione melius; ergo haec

equipped and perfect and complete in all of its aspects and parts. For as Chrysippus says, just as a cover is made for a shield and a sheath for a sword, everything—except the universe—is created for the sake of something else. Thus grains and fruits which grow in the earth are made to nourish living creatures, while animals exist for the sake of humans—the horse for riding, the ox for plowing, the dog for hunting and keeping watch. Humans have emerged for contemplating and imitating the universe. We are certainly not perfect, but we are a part of perfection.

38. "But the universe must be truly perfect since it embraces everything and nothing exists that is not in it. How therefore can it fail to possess that which is best? Nothing is better than intelligence and reason, so the

mundo deesse non possunt. Bene igitur idem Chrysippus, qui similitudines adiungens omnia in perfectis et maturis docet esse meliora, ut in equo quam in eculeo, in cane quam in catulo, in viro quam in puero; item quod in omni mundo optimum sit, id in perfecto aliquo atque absoluto esse debere.

39. "Est autem nihil mundo perfectius, nihil virtute melius; igitur mundi est propria virtus. Nec vero hominis natura perfecta est, et efficitur tamen in homine virtus; quanto igitur in mundo facilius; est ergo in eo virtus. Sapiens est igitur et propterea deus.

Atque hac mundi divinitate perspecta tribuenda est sideribus eadem divinitas; quae ex mobilissima purissimaque aetheris parte gignuntur neque ulla praeterea sunt admixta natura totaque sunt calida atque perlucida,

universe cannot lack these things. Chrysippus illustrates this well by analogies showing that the complete and mature creature is always better—a horse is better than a foal, a dog than a puppy, and a man than a boy. Therefore that which is best in the whole universe must be that which is perfect and complete.

39. "Since nothing can be more perfect than the universe and nothing is better than excellence, the universe must possess excellence. Human nature is not perfect, but excellence may be found in humans. How much more easily then does the universe achieve it! Therefore the universe does indeed possess excellence, being thus wise and, on account of this, divine.

Since we have determined that the universe possesses a divine nature, we must also

ut ea quoque rectissime et animantia esse et sentire atque intellegere dicantur.

40. "Atque ea quidem tota esse ignea duorum sensuum testimonio confirmari Cleanthes putat, tactus et oculorum. Nam solis calor et candor inlustrior est quam ullius ignis, quippe qui inmenso mundo tam longe lateque conluceat, et is eius tactus est, non ut tepefaciat solum, sed etiam saepe comburat, quorum neutrum faceret, nisi esset igneus. 'Ergo' inquit 'cum sol igneus sit Oceanique alatur umoribus' (quia nullus ignis sine pastu aliquo possit permanere)

assign that same divinity to the stars, for they are born from the most moveable and pure part of it—the aether[23]—which is not mixed with anything else. They are by nature a fiery heat and translucent throughout, so that we can rightly say they are living creatures with sensation and intelligence.

40. "That the stars are composed wholly of fire Cleanthes believes is confirmed by two senses, touch and sight. For the heat and radiance of the Sun is more brilliant than any fire, since it shines far and wide over a vast universe. The touch of its rays not only warms but often burns, which would not be the case unless it were made of fire. 'Therefore,' says Cleanthes, 'since the Sun is made of fire and is nourished by the moisture of the ocean'[24]—for no fire

'necesse est aut ei similis sit igni, quem adhibemus ad usum atque victum, aut ei, qui corporibus animantium continetur.

41. "'Atqui hic noster ignis, quem usus vitae requirit, confector est et consumptor omnium idemque, quocumque invasit, cuncta disturbat ac dissipat; contra ille corporeus vitalis et salutaris omnia conservat, alit, auget, sustinet sensuque adficit.' Negat ergo esse dubium horum ignium sol utri similis sit, cum is quoque efficiat, ut omnia floreant et in suo quaeque genere pubescant. Quare, cum solis ignis similis eorum ignium sit, qui sunt in corporibus animantium, solem quoque animantem esse oportet, et quidem reliqua astra, quae oriantur in ardore caelesti, qui aether vel caelum nominatur.

could continuously burn unless it received sustenance—'it must be like the fire we use in everyday life or like the fire that is contained in the bodies of living creatures.'

41. "Cleanthes continues: 'This fire we use in everyday life destroys and consumes all that it touches. Wherever it spreads, it scatters everything and causes chaos. But the heat in our bodies gives life and health. It preserves, nourishes, increases, and sustains all things while providing them with sensation.' He says therefore there is no doubt which of these two kinds of fire the Sun resembles, for it also causes all things to increase and grow, each according to its own kind. Because of this similarity to the fire that resides in all living things, the Sun must also be alive, as must the other heavenly

42. "Cum igitur aliorum animantium ortus in terra sit, aliorum in aqua, in aere aliorum, absurdum esse Aristoteli videtur in ea parte, quae sit ad gignenda animantia aptissima, animal gigni nullum putare. Sidera autem aetherium locum optinent; qui quoniam tenuissimus est et semper agitatur et viget, necesse est, quod animal in eo gignatur, id et sensu acerrumo et mobilitate celerrima esse. Quare cum in aethere astra gignantur, consentaneum est in his sensum inesse et intellegentiam, ex quo efficitur in deorum numero astra esse ducenda. Etenim licet videre acutiora ingenia et ad intellegendum aptiora eorum, qui terras incolant eas, in quibus aer sit purus ac tenuis, quam illorum, qui utantur crasso caelo atque concreto.

bodies, for they arise from that fiery heat of the heavens we call aether or sky.

42. "Since therefore some forms of life are born on land, others in water, and others in the air, it is absurd—so says Aristotle[25]— that no life arises in that part of the universe best suited for giving birth to living things. Now, the stars occupy the region of the aether, a quite rarified realm constantly in lively motion. So if any creature arises there, it must possess the keenest senses and swiftest power of movement. Since stars are born in the aether, logically they must have both sensation and intelligence. From this it follows that the stars must be numbered among the gods. For it is easy to see that those who dwell here on earth in lands where the air is pure and rarified have minds that are sharper and more intelligent than

43. "Quin etiam cibo, quo utare, interesse aliquid ad mentis aciem putant. Probabile est igitur praestantem intellegentiam in sideribus esse, quae et aetheriam partem mundi incolant et marinis terrenisque umoribus longo intervallo extenuatis alantur. Sensum autem astrorum atque intellegentiam maxume declarat ordo eorum atque constantia — nihil est enim, quod ratione et numero moveri possit sine consilio — in quo nihil est temerarium, nihil varium, nihil fortuitum. Ordo autem siderum et in omni aeternitate constantia neque naturam significat — est enim plena rationis — neque fortunam, quae amica varietati constantiam respuit. Sequitur ergo, ut ipsa sua sponte, suo sensu ac divinitate moveantur.

those who live where the air is thick and heavy.

43. "In addition, it is thought that the sharpness of a creature's mind depends on the food it eats. Now, on these grounds it is likely that the stars have extraordinary intelligence since they live in the realm of the aether and are nourished by the vapors of the land and sea which are rarified by the great distance they must travel to reach and sustain them. But what most of all argues that the stars are conscious and intelligent is their order and regularity—for indeed nothing can move in a rational and orderly way without planning—and there is nothing casual, nothing variable, nothing fortuitous in the stars. This systematic order of the heavens through all eternity shows us that their movement is not a random act of

44. "Nec vero Aristoteles non laudandus in eo, quod omnia, quae moventur, aut natura moveri censuit aut vi aut voluntate; moveri autem solem et lunam et sidera omnia; quae autem natura moverentur, haec aut pondere deorsum aut levitate in sublime ferri, quorum neutrum astris contingeret propterea, quod eorum motus in orbem circumque ferretur; nec vero dici potest vi quadam maiore fieri, ut contra naturam astra moveantur, quae enim potest maior esse? Restat igitur, ut motus astrorum sit voluntarius.

Quae qui videat, non indocte solum, verum etiam impie faciat, si deos esse neget.

nature—for it is highly rational—nor mere chance, for chance loves variation and hates regularity. It follows therefore that the stars move of their own free will because of their intelligence and divinity.

44. "We must also praise Aristotle for teaching us that everything which moves must move by nature, force, or will. Now, the Sun, Moon, and stars are clearly in motion. We know that everything moved by nature either falls because of its weight or rises because of its lightness. But neither case applies to the heavenly bodies because their motion is circular. It can scarcely be argued that the stars are made to move by a greater force acting on them contrary to their nature, for what stronger force could there be? The only remaining possibility is that the movement of the stars is by their own will.

Nec sane multum interest, utrum id neget, an eos omni procuratione atque actione privet; mihi enim, qui nihil agit, esse omnino non videtur. Esse igitur deos ita perspicuum est, ut, id qui neget, vix eum sanae mentis existimem."

Anyone who sees this truth and denies it is not only ignorant but guilty of impiety if he says that the gods do not exist. And there is very little difference between denying their existence and depriving them of any stewardship or providential care. For it seems to me that someone who is inactive barely exists at all. To sum up, the existence of the gods is so abundantly clear that I regard anyone who denies it as out of his mind."

SOMNIUM SCIPIONIS

9. Scipio: "Cum in Africam venissem Manilio consule, ad quartam legionem tribunus, ut scitis, militum, nihil mihi fuit potius quam ut Masinissam convenirem, regem familiae nostrae iustis de causis amicissimum. Ad quem ut veni, complexus me senex conlacrimavit, aliquantoque post suspexit ad caelum, et 'Grates' inquit 'tibi ago, summe Sol, vobisque reliqui caelites, quod antequam ex hac vita migro, conspicio in meo regno et his tectis Publium Cornelium Scipionem, cuius ego nomine ipso recreor: ita numquam ex animo meo discedit illius optimi atque invictissimi viri memoria.' Deinde ego illum de suo regno, ille me de nostra re publica percontatus est,

THE DREAM OF SCIPIO

9. As you know, when I[1] had come to Africa as military tribune to the fourth legion while Manilius was consul, my greatest desire was to meet King Masinissa, who was a great friend of my family for the best of reasons.[2] When I came to him, the old man embraced me and wept, then after a little while looked up at the sky and said: "I give thanks to you, most excellent Sun, and to all the other gods in the sky because before I leave this life I have welcomed into my kingdom and my home Publius Cornelius Scipio, whose very name restores my life. The memory of Africanus, that best and most unconquerable man, never departs from my memory." I then asked him about

multisque verbis ultro citroque habitis, ille
nobis est consumptus dies.

10. "Post autem, apparatu regio accepti,
sermonem in multam noctem produximus,
cum senex nihil nisi de Africano loquere-
tur, omniaque eius non facta solum sed
etiam dicta meminisset. Deinde ut cubitum
discessimus, me et de via fessum, et qui
ad multam noctem vigilassem, artior quam
solebat somnus complexus est. Hic mihi—
credo equidem ex hoc quod eramus locuti;
fit enim fere ut cogitationes sermonesque
nostri pariant aliquid in somno, tale quale
de Homero scribit Ennius, de quo videli-
cet saepissime vigilans solebat cogitare et
loqui—Africanus se ostendit, ea forma quae
mihi ex imagine eius quam ex ipso erat no-
tior; quem ubi agnovi, equidem cohorrui;

his kingdom and he asked me about the Roman state, so that the day passed with much conversation between us.

10. After this I dined royally and we talked deep into the night, the old man speaking of nothing but Africanus. Masinissa remembered not only all the things my grandfather had done but also everything he had said. Then finally we went to our beds. I was so exhausted from my journey and from staying up late that I was gripped by a much deeper sleep than usual. In my sleep—and I believe this was a result of our conversation, since our thoughts and words often give birth in sleep to something such as Ennius writes about Homer, of whom he obviously thought and spoke a great deal when he was awake[3]—Africanus appeared. I knew his appearance better from his wax

sed ille 'Ades' inquit 'animo et omitte ti-
morem, Scipio, et, quae dicam trade
memoriae.

11. " 'Videsne illam urbem, quae parere populo Romano coacta per me, renovat pris-
tina bella nec potest quiescere?'—ostendebat
autem Carthaginem de excelso et pleno stellarum, illustri et claro quodam loco—'Ad
quam tu oppugnandam nunc venis paene
miles, hanc hoc biennio consul evertes,
eritque cognomen id tibi per te partum,
quod habes adhuc a nobis hereditarium.
Cum autem Carthaginem deleveris, trium-
phum egeris, censorque fueris et obieris
legatus Aegyptum Syriam Asiam Graeciam,
deligere iterum consul absens, bellumque
maximum conficies: Numantiam exscindes.
Sed cum eris curru in Capitolium invectus,

death-mask than from having seen him.[4] When I recognized him, I began to tremble. But he said: "Be calm, Scipio, and don't be afraid. And remember what I tell you.

11. "Do you see that city, the one I forced to obey the Roman people but which now renews the war and is unable to keep the peace?" He was pointing to Carthage as he stood upon a high place full of stars, both glorious and bright. "You've come to fight against it now as little more than a common soldier, but in two years as consul you will destroy it and earn that name by your own efforts, which you received from me as an inheritance. After you have destroyed Carthage and celebrated your triumph, you will become censor, then ambassador to Egypt, Syria, Asia, and Greece. Following this, you will be elected consul a second time and

offendes rem publicam consiliis perturba-
tam nepotis mei.

12. "'Hic tu, Africane, ostendas oportebit
patriae lumen animi ingenii consiliique tui.
Sed eius temporis ancipitem video quasi fa-
torum viam. Nam cum aetas tua septenos
octiens solis anfractus reditusque conver-
terit, duoque hi numeri—quorum uterque
plenus alter altera de causa habetur—circuitu
naturali summam tibi fatalem confecerint,
in te unum atque in tuum nomen se tota
convertet civitas: te senatus, te omnes boni,
te socii, te Latini intuebuntur; tu eris unus
in quo nitatur civitatis salus, ac ne multa,
dictator rem publicam constituas oportet—si
impias propinquorum manus effugeris.'

conclude a great war by conquering Numantia.[5] But after you have ridden in your triumphal chariot to the Capitol, you will find the Roman Republic in disorder thanks to the plans of my grandson.[6]

12. "This will be the time, Scipio, when you must show your fatherland the brilliance of your mind, your talent, and your judgment. But I see at this point a double path of fate before you. For when your years have reached seven times eight circular revolutions of the Sun, and when these two numbers—which are both considered perfect for different reasons—have by the completion of their circuits fulfilled your fate, to you and to your name the whole state will turn. To you they will all look, the Senate, the leading citizens, the allies, and the Latins. You will be the one person on whom

Hic cum exclamasset Laelius, ingemuis-
sentque vehementius ceteri, leviter arridens
Scipio, 'St! quaeso' inquit, 'ne me e somno
excitetis, et parumper audite cetera.'

13. " 'Sed quo sis, Africane, alacrior ad tut-
andam rem publicam, sic habeto: omnibus
qui patriam conservaverint adiuverint aux-
erint, certum esse in caelo definitum locum,
ubi beati aevo sempiterno fruantur. Nihil
est enim illi principi deo, qui omnem mundum regit, quod quidem in terris fiat, ac-
ceptius, quam concilia coetusque hominum iure sociati, quae civitates appellantur:

the safety of the whole state depends. In short, you will have to restore the Republic as dictator—if you can escape the impious hands of those close to you."[7]

At this point Laelius[8] cried out and the others present groaned deeply. But I laughed gently and said, "Quiet, please, or you'll wake me from my dream. Just listen for a little while to his remaining words."

Then he continued:

13. "Scipio, so that you may be more eager to preserve the Republic, know this: for everyone who has saved, helped, or increased the fatherland, there is a special place set aside in the heavens where they may enjoy blessed eternal happiness. For there is nothing on earth more pleasing to that highest God who rules the whole universe than those councils and gatherings under law of

harum rectores et conservatores hinc pro-
fecti huc revertuntur.'

14. "Hic ego—etsi eram perterritus non
tam mortis metu quam insidiarum a meis—
quaesivi tamen viveretne ipse et Paulus pater,
et alii quos nos exstinctos arbitraremur.

'Immo vero' inquit, 'hi vivunt, qui e cor-
porum vinculis tamquam e carcere evolaver-
unt. Vestra vero quae dicitur vita, mors est.
Quin tu aspicis ad te venientem Paulum
patrem?'

Quem ut vidi, equidem vim lacrimarum
profudi; ille autem me complexus atque
osculans flere prohibebat.

people which are called states. The rulers and preservers of these have set out from here and to here they return."

14. At this point—even though I was afraid not so much of death as I was treachery by those close to me—I asked him whether he and my father Paulus were actually alive, along with those we think of as dead.

"Yes, indeed," he said. "These people are alive and have escaped from the chains of their bodies as if from a prison. For this thing you call life is in fact death. Don't you see your father Paulus approaching you now?"

And I did see him. My eyes were full of tears, but he embraced and kissed me and told me not to cry.

15. "Atque ego ut primum fletu represso loqui posse coepi, 'Quaeso,' inquam, 'pater sanctissime atque optime, quoniam haec est vita, ut Africanum audio dicere, quid moror in terris? Quin huc ad vos venire propero?'

'Non est ita,' inquit ille; 'nisi enim deus is cuius hoc templum est omne quod conspicis, istis te corporis custodiis liberaverit, huc tibi aditus patere non potest. Homines enim sunt hac lege generati, qui tuerentur illum globum quem in hoc templo medium vides, quae terra dicitur; eisque animus datus est ex illis sempiternis ignibus quae sidera et stellas vocatis, quae globosae et rotundae, divinis animatae mentibus, circulos suos orbesque conficiunt celeritate mirabili. Quare et tibi, Publi, et piis omnibus retinendus animus est in custodia corporis, nec iniussu eius a quo ille est vobis datus, ex hominum vita migrandum est, ne

15. As soon as I was able to stop weeping, I began to speak: "Most blessed and best of fathers, since, as Africanus told me, this is life, why should I linger in the world? Why don't I hurry to come here to you?"

"That is not how things work," he said. "Unless God, who rules over all this holy place you see, frees you from guardianship of your body, you cannot come here. Humans are born to obey this law, that they care for the world you see in the middle of this sacred realm, which is called the Earth. They are given souls drawn from those eternal fires you call constellations and stars. These spherical globes are animated with divine minds and complete their rotations and orbits with miraculous speed. And so, Scipio, you and all pious people must keep your souls within the guardianship of your body. You must not depart from your body

munus humanum assignatum a deo defu-
gisse videamini.

16. " 'Sed sic, Scipio, ut avus hic tuus, ut ego
qui te genui, iustitiam cole et pietatem, quae
cum magna in parentibus et propinquis,
tum in patria maxima est: ea vita via est
in caelum et in hunc coetum eorum qui
iam vixerunt, et corpore laxati illum incolunt locum quem vides'—erat autem is
splendidissimo candore inter flammas cir-
cus elucens—'quem vos, ut a Graiis accepis-
tis, orbem lacteum nuncupatis.'

Ex quo omnia mihi contemplanti praeclara
cetera et mirabilia videbantur; erant autem
eae stellae quas numquam ex hoc loco vidi-
mus, et eae magnitudines omnium quas esse
numquam suspicati sumus. Ex quibus erat

without the permission of the one who gave you your soul. You cannot be seen abandoning the earthly duty assigned to you by God.

16. "But like your grandfather here and like me, the one who gave you life, you should cultivate justice and piety. This is of great importance in relation to your parents and family, but most of all to your country. That is the way to come to these heavens and to this gathering of those who now have lived and been freed from their bodies so that they inhabit the place you see"—it was a shining circle bright with a most splendid light among the glowing stars—"which you, as you have learned from the Greeks, call the Milky Way."

As I looked at everything about me, it all seemed marvelous and wonderful. There

ea minima, quae ultima a caelo, citima terris, luce lucebat aliena. Stellarum autem
globi terrae magnitudinem facile vincebant;
iam ipsa terra ita mihi parva visa est, ut me
imperii nostri, quo quasi punctum eius at-
tingimus, paeniteret.

17. "Quam cum magis intuerer, 'Quaeso,'
inquit Africanus, 'quousque humi defixa
tua mens erit? Nonne aspicis quae in templa veneris? Novem tibi orbibus, vel potius
globis, conexa sunt omnia: quorum unus
est caelestis, extimus, qui reliquos omnes
complectitur, summus ipse deus arcens et
continens ceteros, in quo sunt infixi illi qui
volvuntur stellarum cursus sempiterni; cui

were stars we never see from this place and their size was such as we never suspected. The smallest one, which was farthest from the heavens, was closest to the Earth and shone with a borrowed light.[9] The globes of the stars easily surpassed the size of the Earth, while the Earth itself seemed small to me now, so that I was ashamed of our empire that was little more than a point on it.

17. As I continued to look, Africanus asked me: "How long will your mind be fixed on the ground? Don't you see this sacred place to which you have come? Everything you see here is connected in nine circles or rather spheres. One of them, the highest, is the celestial sphere which embraces all the rest. The Supreme God himself protects and sets the limits on the others. In this celestial

subiecti sunt septem qui versantur retro, contrario motu atque caelum. Ex quibus unum globum possidet illa quam in terris Saturniam nominant; deinde est hominum generi prosperus et salutaris ille fulgor qui dicitur Iovis; tum rutilus horribilisque terris quem Martium dicitis; deinde de septem mediam fere regionem Sol obtinet, dux et princeps et moderator luminum reliquorum, mens mundi et temperatio, tanta magnitudine ut cuncta sua luce lustret et compleat. Hunc ut comites consequuntur Veneris alter, alter Mercurii cursus, in infimoque orbe Luna radiis solis accensa convertitur. Infra autem iam nihil est nisi mortale et caducum, praeter animos munere deorum hominum generi datos; supra lunam sunt aeterna omnia. Nam ea quae est media et nona, Tellus, neque movetur et infima est, et in eam feruntur omnia nutu suo pondera.'

sphere the eternal courses of the fixed stars revolve. Inside this are seven spheres which revolve in the opposite direction, contrary to the motion of the heavens. The first of these spheres is that of Saturn, as it called by those in your world. Next is the shining light of Jupiter bringing health and safety to the human race. Then there is the red and hateful sphere which you ascribe to Mars. Placed near the center is the Sun, the leader, ruler, and guide of all the other stars, the mind and organizing force of the universe, so large that it illuminates and fills everything with its light. Finally there are the orbits of Venus and of Mercury, following like attendants. Lowest of all, the Moon in its orbit turns, shining by the rays of the Sun. Below that there is nothing save that which is mortal and transitory, except the souls given to the human race by the gods.

18. "Quae cum intuerer stupens, ut me re-
cepi, 'Quid hic' inquam 'quis est qui com-
plet aures meas, tantus et tam dulcis sonus?'

'Hic est' inquit 'ille qui intervallis coni-
unctus imparibus, sed tamen pro rata parte
distinctis, impulsu et motu ipsorum orbium
efficitur, et acuta cum gravibus temperans
varios aequabiliter concentus efficit. Nec
enim silentio tanti motus incitari possunt, et
natura fert ut extrema ex altera parte graviter,
ex altera autem acute sonent. Quam ob
causam summus ille caeli stellifer cursus,
cuius conversio est concitatior, acuto et ex-
citato movetur sono, gravissimo autem hic

Above the Moon all things are eternal. The ninth sphere,[10] in center of all, is the Earth, which is fixed and does not move. It is the place to which all weights fall by their own will."[11]

18. I was overwhelmed and stared at all of it until I finally recovered myself and asked: "What is that sound, so strong and sweet, that fills my ears?"

"That sound," he said, "arises from the action and motion of the spheres themselves. It is joined together in uneven intervals, but nonetheless divided according to proportion. By blending together high notes with low, a melodious music is created.[12] The movement of the heavenly spheres cannot be silent. The lowest sphere naturally makes a deep sound, while the farthest away makes a high sound. That is, the highest

lunaris atque infimus; nam terra nona im-
mobilis manens una sede semper haeret,
complexa medium mundi locum. Illi autem
octo cursus, in quibus eadem vis est duorum, septem efficiunt distinctos intervallis
sonos, qui numerus rerum omnium fere
nodus est; quod docti homines nervis imi-
tati atque cantibus, aperuerunt sibi reditum
in hunc locum, sicut alii qui praestantibus ingeniis in vita humana divina studia
coluerunt.

19. " 'Hoc sonitu oppletae aures hominum
obsurduerunt, nec est ullus hebetior sensus in vobis; sicut ubi Nilus ad illa quae

sphere bearing the stars of heaven, which turns very rapidly, makes a high and lively sound. The movement of lowest sphere, that of the Moon, causes a deep sound. The ninth sphere, the Earth, is silent and does not move, embracing, as it does, the center of the universe. But the other eight orbits of the spheres, with two having the same pitch,[13] make seven sounds distinct in their intervals—a key number to almost all things that exist. Learned men who have imitated the sound with stringed instruments and voices have opened for themselves a return to this place, just as others with outstanding minds have cultivated divine studies in human life.

19. "The ears of humanity are filled with this sound all the time and are thus grown deaf to it. None of your other senses is more

Catadupa nominantur praecipitat ex altis-
simis montibus, ea gens quae illum locum
accolit propter magnitudinem sonitus sensu
audiendi caret; hic vero tantus est totius
mundi incitatissima conversione sonitus, ut
eum aures hominum capere non possint,
sicut intueri solem adversum nequitis, ei-
usque radiis acies vestra sensusque vincitur.'

20. "Haec ego admirans referebam tamen
oculos ad terram identidem; tum Africanus,
'Sentio' inquit 'te sedem etiamnunc hominum ac domum contemplari; quae si tibi
parva, ut est, ita videtur, haec caelestia semper spectato, illa humana contemnito. Tu
enim quam celebritatem sermonis hominum
aut quam expetendam consequi gloriam

dulled. The same thing has happened in the place called Catadupa,[14] where the Nile plunges down from the mountains. The people who live there have become completely deaf because of the loudness of the sound. Likewise the music of the entire universe rotating rapidly is so loud that human ears cannot hear it, just as you cannot stare directly at the Sun because your sense of sight is overcome by the intensity of its rays."

20. Although I marveled at these heavenly things, I kept turning my eyes back to the Earth. Then Africanus said: "I realize you are still focused on the dwelling and home of humanity, but if you were to realize that it truly is as small as it seems to you, you would turn your sight to heavenly things and scorn human affairs. What kind of praise

potes? Vides habitari in terra raris et angustis in locis, et in ipsis quasi maculis ubi habitatur, vastas solitudine interiectas, eosque qui incolunt terram non modo interruptos ita esse ut nihil inter ipsos ab aliis ad alios manare possit, sed partim obliquos, partim transversos, partim etiam adversos stare vobis: a quibus exspectare gloriam certe nullam potestis.

21. " 'Cernis autem eandem terram quasi quibusdam redimitam et circumdatam cingulis, e quibus duos maxime inter se diversos, et caeli verticibus ipsis ex utraque parte subnixos, obriguisse pruina vides, medium autem illum et maximum solis ardore torreri? Duo sunt habitabiles, quorum australis ille

from the mouths of men or what kind of glory can you achieve in that place that is worthwhile? You can see that humans inhabit only small, narrow parts of the Earth and are scattered about in these, separated by vast wastelands. The inhabitants of your world are so cut off from each other that nothing is able to pass from one group to another. Some live on the same latitude as you, but others below you, and some on the opposite side of the globe. You can certainly not expect to gain fame among them!

21. "You can see that the Earth is bound and girded as if by zones, of which the two most distant from each other lie beneath opposite poles of the sky and are frozen stiff by the cold. The central zone of the Earth is the largest and parched by the heat of the Sun. Only two zones of your world

in quo qui insistunt adversa vobis urgent vestigia, nihil ad vestrum genus; hic autem alter subiectus aquiloni quem incolitis, cerne quam tenui vos parte contingat: omnis enim terra quae colitur a vobis, angustata verticibus, lateribus latior, parva quaedam insula est, circumfusa illo mari quod Atlanticum, quod magnum, quem Oceanum appellatis in terris; qui tamen tanto nomine quam sit parvus vides.

22. " 'Ex his ipsis cultis notisque terris, num aut tuum aut cuiusquam nostrum nomen vel Caucasum, hunc quem cernis transcendere potuit, vel illum Gangem tranatare? Quis in reliquis orientis aut obeuntis solis ultimis aut aquilonis austrive partibus tuum

are habitable, with the southern one, whose inhabitants have their feet opposite from you, completely cut off from your zone. And there, if you look, you will see only a small part of the northern zone belongs to you. The whole land you inhabit is like a little island, narrow from north to south and only somewhat wider east to west. It is surrounded by a sea called the Atlantic or Great Sea or Ocean—but in spite of whatever grand name is used it is really quite small.

22. "And you surely don't believe that your fame or that of anyone among you could be so great as to pass from the lands you know and inhabit to climb the Caucasus Mountains, which you see down there, or swim across the Ganges River over there? No one

nomen audiet? Quibus amputatis cernis profecto, quantis in angustiis vestra se gloria
dilatari velit. Ipsi autem qui de nobis loqu-
untur, quam loquentur diu?

23. "'Quin etiam si cupiat proles illa fu-
turorum hominum deinceps laudes unius-
cuiusque nostrum a patribus acceptas pos-
teris prodere, tamen propter eluviones
exustionesque terrarum, quas accidere tempore certo necesse est, non modo non aeternam, sed ne diuturnam quidem gloriam
adsequi possumus. Quid autem interest,
ab eis qui postea nascentur sermonem fore
de te, cum ab eis nullus fuerit qui ante nati

in the far eastern lands or the remote west or the northern or southern regions will ever so much as hear your name. And if you take those people out of consideration, you will see how tiny is the land across which you hope to spread your glory. Even among those who do know us, how long will your memory last?

23. "Assume for a moment that the children of future generations will indeed want to pass on to their descendants stories praising us that they heard from their fathers. The floods and fires that destroy the earth at regular intervals will inevitably come and wipe out any hope we might have that our glory will last very long, let alone be eternal.[15] But indeed, why do you care that future generations remember you? After all, no one in the past ever spoke

sunt, qui nec pauciores et certe meliores fuerunt viri.

24. "'Praesertim cum apud eos ipsos, a quibus audiri nomen nostrum potest, nemo unius anni memoriam consequi possit? Homines enim populariter annum tantummodo solis, id est unius astri, reditu metiuntur; reapse autem, cum autem ad idem unde semel profecta sunt cuncta astra redierint, eandemque totius caeli discriptionem longis intervallis rettulerint, tum ille vere vertens annus appellari potest, in quo vix dicere audeo quam multa hominum saecula teneantur. Namque ut olim deficere sol hominibus exstinguique visus est cum Romuli animus haec ipsa in templa penetravit, quandoque ab eadem parte sol eodemque tempore iterum defecerit, tum signis omnibus ad principium stellisque revocatis

about you—and they were more numerous than us and better men.

24. "We should also keep in mind that even among those who are able to hear about us, no one will remember us for more than a year. People commonly measure the passage of a year by the Sun, that is, by the cycle of a single star. But a year is in fact measured by the time it takes for all stars in the heavens to return to the place from which they began—and how many human generations that would take I scarcely would dare to say.[16]

Once long ago it seemed to those living on the Earth as if the Sun had failed and its light extinguished, just at the moment the spirit of Romulus ascended into this sacred place. When the Sun reaches that same place again at the same time, then you will know

expletum annum habeto; cuius quidem anni nondum vicesimam partem scito esse conversam.

25. "'Quocirca si reditum in hunc locum desperaveris, in quo omnia sunt magnis et praestantibus viris, quanti tandem est ista hominum gloria, quae pertinere vix ad unius anni partem exiguam potest? Igitur alte spectare si voles atque hanc sedem et aeternam domum contueri, neque te sermonibus vulgi dederis, nec in praemiis humanis spem posueris rerum tuarum, suis te oportet illecebris ipsa virtus trahat ad verum decus. Quid de te alii loquantur, ipsi videant, sed loquentur tamen; sermo autem omnis ille et angustiis cingitur his regionum quas vides, nec umquam de ullo perennis fuit; et obruitur

that the stars have returned to their place of origin and that a year has truly passed. So far not even a twentieth of that time has passed.

25. "And so, even if you despair of returning someday to this place in which all things exist for great and eminent men, what is human glory really worth? After all, it scarcely lasts for even a fraction of a single year. So gaze upward if you will and contemplate this dwelling place and eternal home. Pay no attention to what the common mob might say about you and place none of your hopes in human rewards. Let virtue herself by her own allurements draw you to true honor. Let other people worry over what they say about you—they will say it in any case. All their words are contained

hominum interitu, et oblivione posteritatis exstinguitur.'

26. "Quae cum dixisset, 'Ego vero' inquam 'Africane, si quidem bene meritis de patria quasi limes ad caeli aditus patet, quamquam a pueritia vestigiis ingressus patris et tuis decori vestro non defui, nunc tamen tanto praemio exposito enitar multo vigilantius.'

Et ille, 'Tu vero enitere, et sic habeto, non esse te mortalem, sed corpus hoc; nec enim tu is es quem forma ista declarat, sed mens cuiusque is est quisque, non ea figura quae digito demonstrari potest. Deum te igitur scito esse, si quidem est deus qui viget, qui sentit, qui meminit, qui providet, qui tam regit et moderatur et movet id corpus cui

inside that narrow bit of the Earth you see below you and none of them will last forever. Whatever they say is lost when they die and their words are forgotten by generations yet to come."

26. When he had finished speaking, I said: "Truly, Africanus, if indeed there is a path to the heavens for those who have served their country well, please know that even though I have tried my utmost since boyhood to follow in your footsteps and those of my father and not to fall short of your glory, I will try all the harder now that I see this great reward laid out before me."

And he answered me: "Indeed, keeping striving and know this, that you are not mortal, only your body. You are not what the outward form of your body reveals, not what a finger can point at. The true self of

praepositus est, quam hunc mundum ille princeps deus; et ut mundum ex quadam parte mortalem ipse deus aeternus, sic fragile corpus animus sempiternus movet.

27. " 'Nam quod semper movetur aeternum est; quod autem motum affert alicui, quodque ipsum agitatur aliunde, quando finem habet motus, vivendi finem habeat necesse est. Solum igitur quod sese movet, quia numquam deseritur a se, numquam ne moveri quidem desinit. Quin etiam ceteris quae moventur hic fons, hoc principium est movendi. Principii autem nulla est origo; nam

each person is the mind. Know therefore that you are a god. For a god is someone who moves, who feels, who remembers, who looks to the future, who rules over and guides and directs the body he is master of, just as that Supreme God directs the universe. And just as this eternal God controls the universe, which is partly mortal, so too your eternal spirit directs your fragile body.

27. "That which is always in motion is eternal.[17] But that which causes motion in something else and is itself moved by an external force, when that motion stops it must by necessity cease to live. Therefore only what moves itself, because it never deserts itself, never ceases to move. This then is the source and beginning of movement for all things that move. There is no origin of a

ex principio oriuntur omnia ipsum autem
nulla ex re alia nasci potest; nec enim esset
id principium, quod gigneretur aliunde.
Quodsi numquam oritur, ne occidit quidem
umquam; nam principium exstinctum nec
ipsum ab alio renascetur, nec ex se aliud
creabit, si quidem necesse est a principio
oriri omnia. Ita fit ut motus principium ex
eo sit quod ipsum a se movetur; id autem
nec nasci potest nec mori, vel concidat omne
caelum omnisque natura et consistat necesse
est, nec ullam vim nanciscatur qua a primo
impulsa moveatur.

28. "'Cum pateat igitur aeternum id esse,
quod a se ipso moveatur, quis est, qui hanc
naturam animis esse tributam neget? Inani-
mum est enim omne quod pulsu agitatur

first principle—since a first principle is what all arises from—and so it cannot have originated from anything else. If it arose from something else, it couldn't be called a first principle. If it never starts, then it also never stops. For if the first principle were destroyed, it could not be born again from anything else nor could it create anything from itself, since it is necessary that everything arises from a first principle. Therefore the beginning of motion comes from that which is moved by itself. It cannot be born or die, for otherwise all the heavens and all of nature would by necessity stop, with no force able to move them from the start.

28. "And since it is clear that whatever moves itself is eternal, who can deny that the soul has such a nature? Whatever is moved by an external force is inanimate, but whatever

externo; quod autem est animal, id motu cietur interiore et suo, nam haec est propria natura animi atque vis; quae si est una ex omnibus quae sese moveat, neque nata certe est et aeterna est.

29. " 'Hanc tu exerce in optimis rebus! Sunt autem optimae curae de salute patriae, quibus agitatus et exercitatus animus velocius in hanc sedem et domum suam pervolabit; idque ocius faciet, si iam tum cum erit inclusus in corpore, eminebit foras, et ea quae extra sunt contemplans quam maxime se a corpore abstrahet. Namque eorum animi qui se corporis voluptatibus dediderunt, earumque se quasi ministros praebuerunt—impulsuque libidinum voluptatibus oboedientium, deorum et hominum iura violaverunt—corporibus elapsi circum terram

is animate is moved by its own internal motion. That is the unique nature and power of the soul. And so if it is the one thing of all that moves itself, the nature of the soul is certainly eternal.

29. "So use your soul for the best of deeds! And the greatest deeds of all are done in service to your country. The soul aroused and excited by such deeds will fly more swiftly to this place, its dwelling and home. And it will fly here more quickly if, while it was still entrapped in the body, it has ventured afar and contemplated what lies beyond itself to detach itself from the body as much as possible. Indeed, the souls of those who have given themselves to the pleasures of the body and have made themselves the servants of those pleasures—for those who

ipsam volutantur, nec hunc in locum nisi multis exagitati saeculis revertuntur.'

Ille discessit; ego somno solutus sum."

ruled by such passions and pleasures have broken the laws of gods and men—when they die, circle around the Earth suffering many ages of torment before they return to this place."

Then Africanus departed and I awoke from my sleep.

NOTES

Introduction

1. Available as my own *How to Be a Friend: An Ancient Guide to True Friendship* (Princeton University Press, 2018) and *How to Grow Old: Ancient Wisdom for the Second Half of Life* (Princeton University Press, 2016).

2. One of the many difficulties in translating Cicero is how to render the Latin word *deus*. In cases where Cicero is talking about one of multiple divine beings, I use the lowercase *god* or an equivalent term such as *divinity*. In instances where he clearly means the single supreme Stoic ruler of the universe, I use the uppercase *God*. The various editions of Cicero available show a

wide variety of renderings of the word by thoughtful translators. In any case, readers should keep in mind that whenever the word *God* is used in the following pages, Cicero—though he certainly knew about the teachings of the Jews—naturally had no notion of the later Christian use of the word.

ON THE NATURE OF THE GODS

1. The Academics, represented here by the Roman politician and priest Cotta, claimed descent from the Academy of Plato and approached religious certainty with suspicion, arguing that respectful skepticism regarding divine matters was the best way to live. In the first book of *On the Nature of the Gods*, Velleius presented the case for the teachings of the Epicurean philosophers, followed by a withering critique of these ideas by Cotta.

Balbus will now argue for the Stoic views on the divine.

2. One of the earliest Latin poets, Ennius was often viewed by the Romans with the same awe as Homer among the Greeks. His work from the early second century BC survives only in fragments.

3. Creatures of ancient mythology, the hippo-centaurs were horses with human torsos while a Chimaera was a mixture of different animals, usually a lion with a goat sprouting from its back and a tail ending in the head of a snake.

4. In 496 BC.

5. Perses, king of Macedon, was defeated by the Romans at Pydna on the Aegean coast in 168 BC in the Third Macedonian War. The younger Vatinius was a lieutenant of Julius Caesar. His grandfather was apparently returning to the city after presiding over law courts in the Sabine town of Reate in the mountains just northeast of Rome.

6. A battle in southern Italy dating to about 560 BC. Olympia is in southern Greece.

7. Mopsus is probably the seer who accompanied Jason and the Argonauts on their voyage. Teiresias is the famous blind prophet of Thebes often featured in Greek epic and tragedy. Amphiaraus was a seer from Argos who joined the war of the Seven against Thebes. Calchas was the prophet who accompanied the Greeks to Troy, while Helenus prophesied on the Trojan side.

8. Publius Claudius and Lucius Junius, whose ships were wrecked off of Sicily, were Roman consuls in 249 BC fighting the Carthaginians. The chickens were kept on board Roman ships for use in oracles. If they ate the sacred grain, it was considered a good omen in the battle to come.

9. Coelius Antipater was an early Roman historian who wrote about the Second Punic War against Hannibal. The consul Flaminius

and his army suffered a massive defeat by Hannibal at Lake Trasimene north of Rome in 217 BC.

10. This is one of two versions told by Cicero of the story of the augur Attus Navius, who lived in the early days of Rome's kings. In the other (*De divinatione* 1.31), he vowed the largest bunch of grapes in his vineyard to the Lares spirits if they would help him find his pig.

11. This devotion was a solemn religious act of offering up one's life to the gods before a battle as a sacrifice for the nation, such as Publius Decius Mus did before the Battle of Sentinum against the Gauls in 295 BC.

12. In 162 BC.

13. Cleanthes, a former boxer, succeeded Zeno as head of the Stoic school in third-century BC Athens.

14. In 87 BC the consul Gnaius Octavius, a supporter of Sulla, lost his life fighting against

the forces of his fellow-consul Cinna, a supporter of Marius.

15. In 129 BC Publius Scipio Africanus died suddenly under suspicious circumstances.

16. Chrysippus was a leading Stoic philosopher in third-century BC Athens.

17. Elsewhere (*De fato* 7), Cicero maintains that the Athenians with their clear skies are smarter than the Thebans who live in a cloudy climate.

18. Xenophon *Memorabilia* 1.4.8.

19. The Stoic idea that we derive these qualities of our bodies from the four elements comes from Plato (*Timaeus* 42).

20. Zeno of Citium on the island of Cyprus lived just after the time of Alexander the Great and founded the Stoic school of philosophy, which Balbus argues for here.

21. Cicero's source for these ideas is probably Aristotle (*History of Animals* 8.1; *Parts of Animals* 4.7).

22. *Timaeus* 89.

23. Also called the upper air or the region of the heavens.

24. A common early Greek idea, though Aristotle says it is wrong (*Meteorology* 2.2).

25. From a lost book. Plato expresses the same idea (*Timaeus* 40).

THE DREAM OF SCIPIO

1. Scipio Africanus the Younger (185/4–129 BC).

2. Manius Manilius was consul in 149 BC and in command of the Roman army besieging Carthage in the Third Punic War. Masinissa was a king of Numidia, an ally of Rome, and friend to the elder Scipio Africanus— adoptive grandfather of this Scipio—in the Second Punic War at the end of the previous century. Masinissa died in 149 BC at about the age of ninety.

3. The Roman poet Ennius reported in his *Annals* that Homer once appeared to him in a dream and proclaimed that the Latin writer was a reincarnation of himself.

4. Scipio was only a young child when Africanus died.

5. Scipio destroyed this Spanish city in 133 BC.

6. Tiberius Gracchus.

7. Scipio never in fact became dictator.

8. Laelius, who was present at the narration of the dream, was Scipio's best friend.

9. The Moon.

10. All educated people in the Greek and Roman world knew the Earth was a sphere, not flat.

11. In Cicero's cosmos of nine spheres, the first and outermost celestial sphere contains the fixed stars and turns from east to west. Below that are seven spheres—Saturn, Jupiter, Mars, the Sun, Venus, Mercury, the

Moon—turning from west to east. In the center of the universe is the ninth sphere, the unmoving Earth.

12. The idea of the music of the spheres goes back at least to Plato and probably originates with Pythagoras.

13. Venus and Mercury.

14. Catadupa ("Thundering Falls" in Greek) is the First Cataract of the Nile River at Syene (Aswan).

15. The Stoics believed in periodic destruction of the Earth by flood and fire.

16. The idea of the Great Year originated among the Greeks, if not earlier, and is variously reckoned, among the many estimates, at 3000, 12,954, and 36,000 solar years. Cicero places the beginning of one Great Year at the apotheosis of Romulus, founder of Rome, traditionally dated to the late eighth century BC. If not even a twentieth of that time has

passed between the death of Romulus and the setting of this dialogue in 129 BC, then the Great Year in Cicero's mind must have been at least 11,700 solar years long.

17. This and the following section are a translation of Plato's *Phaedrus* 245C–246A.

FURTHER READING

Everitt, Anthony. *Cicero: The Life and Times of Rome's Greatest Politician*. New York: Random House, 2001.

Gruen, Erich. *The Last Generation of the Roman Republic*. Berkeley: University of California Press, 1995.

Rawson, Elizabeth. *Cicero: A Portrait*. London: Bristol Classical Press, 1983.

Scullard, H. H. *From the Gracchi to Nero: A History of Rome from 133 BC to AD 68*. New York: Routledge, 1982.

Syme, Ronald. *The Roman Revolution*. Oxford: Oxford University Press, 2002.